Winning Back America

How Did We Get Here?

COCRA Publishing

815 W Harbor Dr S, St Petersburg, FL 3370547

Dear reader: this book will acknowledge where we are, and address ways to get back what we—US citizens—have lost. Lost to leftists that want to turn the country into a socialist/communist state, and to invaders who want to install a sharia, ayatollah controlled country.

Before going into ways of regaining control, and bringing back true American Spirit—there will be a brief section on just how we came to this point.

Winning Back America is written to be precise, and direct . Do not get bogged down in the number of pages or words—or lack thereof. There is no padding, no puffery. Why take 300 pages to say what you can in 60?

How Did We Get Here?

Unless you have blinders on, you know the current state of America, specifically the United States of America. A country divided.

Students in college and high school have no respect for the US flag, often burning or stepping on it. Caucasian Americans are called racist, and Nazi—often by other caucasians, who have been taught to be self-loathing.

The media openly supports socialist ideas, champions "people of color"--whether they have qualifications or not. Alas, African-Americans, Hispanic Americans or Asian Americans who do not support the leftist agenda are attacked as being traitors.

Members of Congress spend most of their time championing supposed rights of illegal aliens and refugees, while ignoring actual children, homeless that are US

Citizens.

Muslims have gained a "victim" and "special" class by

the media. We have muslim congressmen who openly hate

the United States, and openly say they are here to install

sharia—and their party, and the media cheer them on... as

do university students, high school students.

Capitalism is, to people under 45, an evil system.

Marxist theories, no matter that they have proven to be

wrong and devastating—are hailed as the way to go.

Thugs wearing masks and brandishing weapons are

allowed to attack those who don't agree with their views—

cheered on by one major political party and the media.

Women are encouraged to come forward with unproven

and, in most cases—obvious false abuse charges. And, if

you ask, "where's the proof?" You are vilified in the press, subject to physical violence.

We have let a few companies garner control of what news and opinions we are allowed to see. That these companies were started by, and controlled by people who came out of the "America is bad. Socialism is good. Muslims are victims" university system—has all but assured that only that particular view point will see the light of day.

That, in the proverbial nutshell is where we are. But, how did we get to this point?

The Cultural / Love Revolution

Travel back in time to the late '60's, early '70's. The country is beginning to go into turmoil. To the positive: the fight for equal rights is on the verge of being won. To the negative: there is an all out assault on "old America."

The seeds are being sewn.

The hippie/flower children movement not only starts, it steams rolls across the universities and high schools. The rush to disavow any morals, mores of your parents, is now the rule.

The war in Vietnam is being broadcast by the news channels: ABC, CBS, and NBC as an immoral and "illegal" action. For the first time, the media is going full tilt anti-American. The young people follow. Open hostility to the country is being shown on college campuses and high schools.

Marxist theory is being embraced. Che, a hatchet man for Fidel Castro, is hailed as a freedom fighter and a hero. Students today, have once again embraced this man—a man who killed people who did not bow to his views, and openly killed gays—as a hero.

Hollywood rushed in to make anti-war movies. Celebrities, non more so than Jane Fonda, railed on about the heroic Viet Cong . Though this should not have been too much of a surprise, Hollywood had a history of supporting leftist movements—in the '30's and '40's, and '50's—until the McCarthy hearings—celebrities freely supported the Soviet Union.

Not to be outdone—the music industry pushed anti-war, anti-American songs. Any singer, song writer or artist who cared for the country, who still believed in traditional America, was shunned.

While this was going on, in the political and entertainment communities. Another, so called revolution was going on. The revolution to do away with cultural, religious norms. Free love was the mantra. Marriage?

Who needed that? Sex was something to be shared and spread about like so much Halloween candy.

Now, what exactly did these movements have to do with the state of today? Good question. Let's look at the years since, and you will see the answer.

The Civil Rights Movement

The Civil Rights Movement was a much needed, and long over due nod to freedom, and truly achieving the American way, the American Dream. No person should be judged by the color of his skin. (Remember that)

Ending segregation was a goal, making things equal became a be all—end all. To that end, we came to start busing... busing that took students from inferior schools and moved them to historically better schools, but, conversely, it took children from those well anointed institutions and bused them to the poorer schools. Instead of fixing the poor performing schools, the wisdom of the courts was the minority students take precedence...

The next step was to penalize one race, in order to "make a level playing field" for another race. Perhaps a good thing in the beginning. But, affirmative action programs soon became entitlements.

Fast forward to 2015, and now, the US has come a full 360... yes, 360, not 180. Minorities now demand, and universities are all too eager to acquiesce, separate dorms, graduations, and "safe places" for themselves—places where no white students are allowed. Curiously, the national , and local media outlets all hail this as the right step, and, an emboldened accomplishment.

The Break Down of the Nuclear Family

Throughout the, in historical context, short existence of the United States, and owing a lot to the roots in Northern Europe, the family was important. The family came together for dinner/supper, and, while enjoying the meal, discussed the day's events. Problems, and victories were gone over here. The family, in most cases, consisted of a father, a mother and the children. This was the norm.

Fathers were involved in their child's schooling and his/her extracurricular activities—as was the mother. Kids not only respected their parents, they looked up to them. Parents took pride in their children.

Once the late '60's came about, a change began to take hold. The family was portrayed in the movies, on TV as a broken, unnecessary institution. For every *"The Waltons,"* there were three or four "*All In the Family*," types that portrayed the Father (particularly a Caucasian Father) as a bigot, a racist, an idiot, uncaring—or all of those things. It became the model—families were broken, Dad's were relics of yesterday.

Soon you had shows with a single woman lead, often a single mother lead. Men were shown to be dumb, or not needed. Families were not shown at all.

This came to take hold in reality, too. The absent father has become not only common, but in some groups, the norm. Men having children and never connecting, or supporting them.

Once the '90's hit—the family, as a functioning unit was all but extinct. Even the ones with a Mother and a Father, lacked a cohesion, purpose: there was no family dinner, no family outing, no family meetings.

And where are we now? The family, says the left, and is nodded to, by that one major party and the media, is a racist, patriarchal construct to impose slavery on women. Huh?

The War On Christianity

One has to rewind back to the cultural, and/or *love* revolution of the '60's/'70's, to see the beginnings of the hatred, loathing that has now come to be common place when discussing Christianity.

The leaders of the new generation, had a disdain for religion in general, all forms. The singers, bands, and actors that were *gods* to a generation, preached: free love;

nothing is immoral; if it feels good—do it; religion is an out of time, out of place conspiracy to limit your mind and experiences.... and, the media of the day, seeing ratings and dollars—went with it.

Soon, you had a generation of babies having babies. The vast majority of whom were unmarried. (Marriage is just a way for *the Man* to hold you back and control you) Most either lived with their parents – a new norm that would take root-- or found themselves on public assistance. Another commonality—the disconnect with the Church.

By now this new generation, the new moms/young women and the young men, had bought into the songs they were hearing, the *leaders* that were on the talks shows, the movies that said the church, religion was passe . They stopped going to Church.

As an adjoiner : where were the parents of these lost young people?

Not only did they turn their backs on religion in general, Christian Churches in particular—they raised their kids to do likewise. The phrase, that was repeated, like so much brainwashed mantra was: *"I am going to let them decide for themselves if they want to go to church."* The kids were set before the TV to watch cartoons on Sunday. On the occasion that Gramps or Granny did come over to collect them for a service, mom reiterated that it was their choice... now, you must remember that these tykes were seeing the same shows, listening to the same *leaders* that said church was bad.

Fast forward: those kids, who never went to church and have been raised to belittle the preacher, the priest, the padre—now have kids. Their kids never were exposed to any positive religious experience, because mom, nor dad had any, nor do they have any desire for their kids to have any.

Now, as this second generation is growing up, they are exposed to *leaders* who are starting to express hatred and disdain for Christianity. The media, and Hollywood start subtly snubbing, and showing the Christian Church, and Christians themselves, as *bible thumpers, out of touch, and evil.* Movies such as: *The Canterbury Tales; The Boys of St Vincent; Footloose; Carrie; Dogma; The Name of The Rose* were becoming the norm, and talked up by the newly popular TV *Entertainment* shows.

By the time of the late '90's another generation was taking hold. Brought up with no religion, and an ever growing disrespect and loathing of Christianity, the attack on the Church became mainstream.

Come 2008 you had the Democratic Party, the new President declaring that *"we are not a Christian Nation."*

This, of course, was parroted by the media wonks—who by now belonged to that second generation that grew up with no respect for any church, and a distrust, loathing of all things Christian. At this time, the traditional Christmas Tree became a *Holiday Tree.*

The democrats, the media, the President said this was done to be *inclusive,* but—to whom? There is no other holiday that falls on December 25th, every year. The *every year*, I added because the wonks love to yell, "Hanukkah." Yes, on occasion, Hanukkah does coincide with Christmas, but not often. I would, and do , challenge the screamers to name a Rabbi that is against Christmas being celebrated with all of it's traditions. They cannot.

No, this is a well thought out attack on Christianity and on the traditions of the United States. Used to pave the way for a leftist take over. And here you have two factions, while each wants their version a new America (the leftists want socialism, the newly emboldened—and playing the victim card—muslims who want to turn the US into a ayatollah controlled islamic desert), they both agree that Western Civilization must end.

The newly elected muslim President took full control of the Democratic party. The party made sure to install friendly trolls in key spots to influence the media—which wasn't hard, as the new *journalists* grew up disliking all things that were traditional to their grandparent—people that they really didn't know, anyway.

By the time a new President was elected in 2016, the Democratic Party, and the media were brazen. When this Republican President started making appointments, the Democrats started using a religious litmus test. Specifically an anti-Christian test.

In particular, Senators Feinstein and Sanders railed on about *dogma*, and how a Christian's views would make them inappropriate for holding a national office. Mind you, neither senator has ever expressed this same sentiment regarding a muslim. In fact, both have defended muslim congressmen when they have made anti-Semitic and anti-American statements.

We now are in an America where talk show hosts openly mock Christianity, saying members of the religion are crazy. Where politicians and the media refer to Christians as *Easter Worshipers...*

The Breaking of a Race

Back when the cultural/sexual revolution began, the mid '60's, there came a movement within a movement. That movement was to, in effect, mock, demean, and demoralize one race—the Caucasian Race.

Why? Several reasons. The main one for here is simple —power. Caucasians were the largest group in the United States, and the ones who built, what the vogue of the day said was an evil, corrupt country. Whites were collectively —*the Man.*

The entertainment industry was then, as it today, a money machine. It makes trends, when it can, and it jumps onto, exploits trends as they develop. In no time at all Hollywood and TV started the downgrading of the American White Male.

We had TV talk shows stating that there was no "white" culture. That white America stole everything.

In movies and TV shows the white male was now portrayed as one of, or a combination of the following: racist, stupid, evil, incompetent, thief, or corrupt.

The white female was portrayed as a more, seeking of bettering herself, by becoming open to the *right* cultures and movements.

By the time the '80's arrived TV shows and movies, where a white female character was a lead or of any importance, she was shown to have a minority boyfriend— usually black, but on occasion—American Indian, or Asian.

Commercials were blatant... the *Advil* commercial of several years back: a group of well dressed white men and women are agonizing over the headache medicines... they couldn't understand the difference. They were lost, until—drum roll, please! A black woman shows up and tells them to just buy the *Advil*! There was a *Sprite* commercial broadcast in Europe: a blonde, white model type female is on her knees performing fellatio on a black male—when he discharges into her mouth, she equates it to *Sprite*.

School books, from Kindergarten through High School, glorified the experience and wisdom of minorities, and down played achievements of white Americans, or historical figures.

History being taught in schools, went from the Founding Fathers, and the hardships of building the greatest civilization ever known, to championing socialist governments. Cuba, was a country being wronged by America. Karl Marx was the new Homer. Che Guevara, a murderous, bigot—was taught to children as a hero... a man who fought the evil forces of colonization.

Throughout the '90's, and still going on, history was being revised. Western Civilization was the root cause of all evils. Whites, AKA Northern Europeans were colonizers who exploited, and enslaved others. Not taught, that Europeans did not enslave the blacks that were brought to North America—these people were enslaved by other blacks (during tribal warfare, the winners sold losers as slaves), and by the muslims of North Africa and the Middle East.

Also not taught, and not vilified: the arguably most successful, and definitely the most brutal colonizers the wold has ever known—the muslim Ottomans. The Ottomans conquered and controlled the Middle-East, North Africa, and part of Europe. They were brutal. You converted or you were killed. They enslaved. It wasn't until a decade into the 20th Century that the Ottoman empire was defeated. Just about 100 years ago, that is all.

Also, never taught, nor mentioned in the media: white, mostly Christian Europeans were enslaved by muslims by the tens of thousands. That—depending upon the scholar—the first slaves to arrive on the shores of what is now the United States, were Irish children.

No, the education system that came into power, the educators that worked in the United States, were decidedly socialist and against traditional Americana.

After the election of President Obama, an all out assault came down to portray white America bereft of all morality, and legitimacy.   White America was racist.

And, of course, the media, now full of self-loathing caucasians, entitled minorities, and haters of Western Civilization—started the great *White Privilege* campaign.

White people only became successful because of the color of their skin. This was taught as fact in schools. Hammered into audiences by the media. Never mind that there are : Miss Black America; Black Entertainment Network; Affirmative Action Programs; minority only scholarships to universities; Black Congressional Caucus, US Hispanic Chamber of Commerce; Hispanic National Bar Association.. etc, and etc...

Come to today: you can be proud to be Black; Hispanic; Asian; Native American. However, if you are proud of being of Northern Europe ancestry—you are racist; Nazi, bigot. If you are muslim—you are regarded as a victim of racist whites. Christian—you are evil, a Nazi.

A person of color is now the phrase that minorities and the media are hammering into the country's psyche. A person of color is, automatically, right. A person of color cannot be racist, no matter what they say or write. A person of color is, automatically—again, more intelligent, and better equipped to make decisions. Any political election, or contest lost by a person of color to a white person, was only lost due to racism, white privilege, and/or cheating.

Now, universities are making *safe places*, where that person of color can go without having to share space with a white person. That person of color now gets his or her own, segregated graduation ceremony, again, so they won't have to be sullied by the presence of a white person. But!

But, a white person cannot have a white only space, nor can they have white only ceremonies. That would be racist.

These points are being driven by not only the news media, but by the entertainment industry, too. Celebrities tell white people to *"shut the fuck up,"* when talking about racial themes, or instances of racial attacks, bigotry—once again, if you are white (now) you cannot be racially discriminated against, nor can an attack on you by a person of color be racial..

Because this self-loathing has been taught, hammered on for decades... you have an entire generation or two of whites, who openly consider themselves as inferior, not worthy of questioning a person of color.

Why has this come about?.. A joint process by socialists and islamic organizations. It started with the socialist movement—in later years, the muslim brotherhood (along with their branches in other parts of the world, ex: CAIR, in North America) joined with dollars and programs. Now, the socialists could only take on as an ally, and champion islamic goals—if islam was a victim...

In the 2016 presidential race, a new word was coined *islamaphobe.* Anyone, especially a white person, who said anything about muslims—was an islamaphobe. Anyone who mentioned that the people who just committed a murderous act, was muslim, ex: the Orlando night club massacre—was an islamaphobe, a racist.

Yes, the media and the Democratic Party of the US-- along with Merkle's party in Germany, and May's in England—convinced everyone that islam / muslim was a race! Of course if you pointed out that muslim are varying colors, and pointed out the obvious, that islam, like any other religion—was a mind set, a set of rules, a thought process—you were branded a racist, and, of course—an islamaphobe.

The Destruction of the American Male

In an ever increasing assault on all things that make Western values, in general, and American in particular, good—the leftists, now in control of the Democratic Party, took aim. The very essence of what has made Western Civilization the greatest civilization ever. The American/Western male. The warriors that saved the world of becoming a Nazi nightmare, that shaped the greatest society the world has known.

There have always been homosexuals. Largely, before, they, as most secure and respectful people have—kept their exploits to themselves. Decency was a thing to be admired. Just as no one wanted to listen to a cretin tell of how many women he had bagged—no one wanted to hear a homosexual go on about their trophies, either.

Still, theirs was a society seen as being abhorrent, or one consisting of mentally ill persons.

This really did not sit well with the producers, writers, actors of hollywood. If hollywood is eighty or ninety percent Jewish, it is also fifty or sixty percent homosexual. So, hollywood's power brokers, by now all too sure that they could not only change, but shape a population's sense of what is real—set out to make homosexuals the norm.

Thus we had *Will and Grace*. A show that would have went nowhere, save the fact that the main character, and the smart, cool one, was homosexual. Of course the media, and the talk shows fawned all over it... Anyone who said the show was lackluster was now branded a bigot...

This is where things started. The seeds of emasculating the Western male in general, and the American male, in particular were sewn.

Soon movies and TV shows were flush with gay characters who were: the smartest, the coolest, the funniest. And, the victim. The victim of the evil white male. Often it was the evil, white, Christian male.

Still, for all of their gains, it plateaued.... Yes, they made gains. Were thought of as the innocents who were victimized. But they were not considered normal by the mainstream.

Then, around 2008, things really amped up. A new president came in. A new era began. The new president, a media darling—he wasn't white (well, actually, though he, nor his supporters or the media, would never admit it, he was as much caucasian as he was black)--had an agenda. To start the transformation of the United States, from a Democratic Republic, to islamic dictatorship.

An over step? No. That president immediately put in

muslim advisers. Under his watch, a concerted effort was set forth to make homosexuals not just a protected class, but *the class*. Out of this came the rise of the totally false notion that there is such a thing as a *trans*-gender. Out of this came parades where naked (but for jock straps) guys could dance down the street, people with dildos glued to themselves could mingle with kids, and it was covered by the press as a much needed step in the right direction.

But, there was still those pesky white males that had to be dealt with...So, along comes the Martin case... and this president declares the white man (don't pay attention to the fact that Zimmerman said of himself—I am Hispanic) guilty—and so does the press. He sends in the DOJ and special prosecutors to ensure that a guilty verdict is rendered. News networks falsify tapes, do edits to make the defendant appear guilty. After a jury decides, correctly, that Martin was the aggressor, another case comes along. The Ferguson case. Again, this president paints the white cop as guilty. He sends (black) DOJ and congressional officials to the funeral. The media again declares the defendant a racist... but, once again, the facts do not fit.

But the damage was done. The media was now fully in the DNC's pocket. Caucasians had been hit with a heavy brush of racism—and the entertainment community, and the news departments all exclaimed—white males are evil.

Which brings us to where we are.

Is it too late to bring about the American Spirit, once more?

No.

But, how to do it?

Quick Fix—Long Term

Now, a look at ways to turn this slide around. A way to bring some sanity back to our culture. Ways to stop the muslim brotherhood's gains. A way, or ways to get a viewpoint, other than the left's out there.

Remember: baby steps. This is going to be a long and protracted fight. But one we have to win. Even though the ultimate goal seems far away, and steps must be taken to reach it—one must not give short thrift to what is going on, now.

We--those who love the *American Way,* traditions of these United States of America—have lost the narrative. More so, surrendered it. Whether you are a conservative, a republican, a democrat, Christian, Jewish, atheist—you have let those that hate Western values, hate the United States control the messages that are being put out there.

This was done by your, our, not speaking up. By our ignoring what was being taught in classrooms from kindergarten through graduate schools. By not calling out those that started disparaging our traditions, our ways of life. By *turning the other cheek.* No, we didn't lose the narrative, the country's voice—we gave it away.

And, to win back the country, we have to start getting our message out there. We have to make sure our viewpoint is being heard, shared. We have to get in the discussion.

At the moment the leftists, the muslim brotherhood have control of the media. Control of the campuses.. and, they are using it to their advantage. Soros, the muslim controlled U.N., and members of the last presidential administration are jointly setting the course.

They do this by organizing scripted demonstrations, by getting the media hacks to be there to tape (and edit) the scenes. They hire people to yell down conservatives at town hall meetings, to get universities to cancel or impose restrictions on conservative speakers, to ambush—with the media just happening to be there—conservatives at airports, restaurants.

So far, conservatives have run, hidden--to the leftists, cowered--all of which has emboldened them, and hardened their resolve.

We cannot keep running, turning the other cheek, letting

ourselves be silenced. But the answer is not to scream

back at the mobs.

It is to turn the tables. To get into the discussion. To

control the message, itself.

"Nazi? I?.. Tell me, when did the Nazi's take over their

country? Do you know what their platform was?" Of

course they do not. History is not being taught in schools,

it is being re-written. "Perhaps, you should talk to a

Holocaust survivor, before letting loose of the term."

Turn the attacks back on them. They have glass jaws.

Their ideas, platform is a house of cards, will fall in the

winds of reason, and fact. It has to, for it has no substance.

But you have to stop being silenced!

Go to meetings. Go to events. Socialize with people,

let them know , in a calm, precise manner, what your

values, your viewpoints are. Do not back down, stay calm,

and keep the control.

If interviewed by a TV news person, a vlogger, a member of the other side, and they keep asking the same question (because they are stuck trying to get their point across): "I just answered that, why are you asking the question, again?" or, "I answered your question, which word confused you?" or, "Oh.. is that what they are teaching in journalism classes, today—if you don't like the answer, you just keep asking the same question? That you should interrupt your guest, when you don't like their answer? Hmm? That's kind of sad," then smile at them... "Really? Rudeness, is the new journalism?"

Refuse to buckle. Sarah Huckabee Sanders was a master of handling rude reporters. Pull up a few of her press conferences and study them.

Keep the calm. Keep your smile. Stay on point.

Ways to get the message out there:

Programs, Field Trips

When a country, when a people lose their faith in their culture, their history—it creates a vacuum. And when that happens, history has shown that another culture will step in--"yes, your past was evil, it was unworthy... come with us, we will show you the light..." Islam is a master of this, and it's their tactic of choice, now.

Just look at Germany—the elite class, decided that neither socialism nor democracy interested them any longer, so they gave away their country. Why? The elite that runs Germany, had long pushed programs to cast away the traditions of the county. The people lost all of their national identity. But in so doing, the ruling class , itself, lost it's sense of national pride.

Most of them had, or had family that had, ties to muslim companies. The muslim leaders, seeing an opening to conquer Europe, made deals. Deals to have tens of thousands of muslim men get refugee status in Germany. And once there, mosques sprang up, no go zones sprang up, police were taught to throw in jail anyone who *insulted* islam.

But why would they make a deal to turn the country over to a culture that would strip away their rights? Because the German rulers think of themselves as so powerful, so needed by the new masters of the country, that they and their families will be immune and to hell with anyone else.

This is what has happened or is on the verge of happening in the United States. Our school systems has taught two generations to have no respect for the county. Indoctrinated them to do away with the country's history, and to re-write it.

This has to be stopped , or the United States will cease to exist.

To that end, and, it will cost time and money, we need to show the next generations that the American Dream, the American Way is superior, and something to be proud of.

You, your companies, your groups—start field trips for grade schoolers, middle schoolers, and yes, high schoolers. Take them to history museums, to historical sites.

Make sure text books are not socialist bent, propaganda, by creating text books for all schools—and pressure school districts, universities to buy, and implement them.

Start extracurricular programs—sports, and educational.

Answer questions, give some insight to the greatness of our country, but be gentle, don't preach. Show them how under the capitalist system they can make a living, grow their passion—and contrast that with how, under a socialist system, the government will own their product, idea, and how it is distributed. Make sure the programs are about, for the kids, that they have fun. It has been shown that more is learned—and retained—during play than rout repetition.

We have to make this new set of children realize how unique and how special the American experience is.

Offer scholarships to conservative, Pro-American colleges—there are still some out there... Give these colleges special attention. Help grow them.

Control of Education

I cannot express just how important the local school systems are. These are the ones that hire the teachers, buy the text books for the K—12 children. They control the voice that will guide, mold these young minds.

For coming on three generations, the left has controlled the local systems. While local conservative groups have been focused on state or national offices, they have let the future be decided by others.

You must run qualified (actually, in most school board races, the qualifications listed are nothing more than sound bites) candidates in each district. In this environment, it is best not to come off as being conservative. Lie? No, of course not. Just frame yourself, or your candidate in a different way. I would suggest that you, the local political group, run at least three candidates in any district race.

If your area does not allow for party affiliation in local races, i.e. school boards, city/town councils, then just run your slate, without the party defined.

In any race that allows for party identification, your organization must run at least three candidates in every district, or every office race. Two under your party, Republican. And one as a Democrat.

Running a camouflaged candidate works in two ways. In the first way, it muddies the other party's primary—draws away votes from the party's most powerful candidate. But you must make sure your disguised candidate is a Republican at heart, and will, if he/she wins, vote with the party. The Democrats have been doing this, successfully, for years.

By winning the majority of local school board seats, we will be able to set the curriculum for the next generation(s). This, I cannot stress enough—is imperative. If the United States is to survive, it must have children who respect and appreciate the liberty that the country affords them, children who will grow into adults who will protect their country.

To make this work, local school boards, colleges, and universities will need text books that are congruent with our conservative, the United States is a worthy country, perspective.

The text books that are being used now teach everything from socialism is good, to the disastrous common core, to homosexual perspective, to white privilege. What they don't focus on is the country's grand history, it's being the leader in the industrial revolution, it's leadership.

This is a crucial step in controlling the narrative. It will take putting the investment into putting out the text books themselves, and marketing them.

Control the Message, Control the Thoughts

At this point in time, a handful of corporations control what is presented to the United States public as news, as entertainment and what is appropriate to view. *Google, Twitter*, and *FaceBook* decide what is news relevant, and what ideas you are allowed to have. *Disney, Amazon, Netflix*, mainly, but hollywood, in general, do their best to transform the country by whom and what they portray in a positive light. While *Amazon* also does it's best to control thought, by refusing to sell books that are not of a leftist bent.

So far the conservative response has been one of moral indignation, and fits of *woe is me*. Employing a trying to sneak content in, or complain loudly to a deaf ear. Oddly enough, Republicans in Congress, Presidency have not brought about a forceful response, ex: anti-trust action.

Since the government will not act, it up to we—the citizens who love traditional America to carry the fight. To regain the narrative.

The key players in social media, *FaceBook* and *Twitter,* do not hide their bias. Their disdain for anyone who does not hold the Soros/UN/muslim/gay destruction of the West goal, is evident. When a complaint is lodged, unless he aggrieved person is a celebrity or national figure, it goes nowhere.

There is a need for someone, some group to make a new, the *next thing* social media platform. Not just a replacement, but an advancement. Ones that will not just highlight conservative points, but would allow a free flow of information. Striving to present news without a bias.

The reasons for there not being conservative outlets so far? It is too hard to create a new platform, especially with *FaceBook* and *Twitter* having such a head start.

Poppycock. Zuckerberg started *FaceBook* in 2004, just some fifteen years ago. *Twitter*? Two years later.

The other excuse that is often expressed: all of the techies are leftists.

This is probably 95% to 99% true. So what? No one said it would be easy. It is just said that it is a necessity. With the right amount of funding and the right approach, a capable team could be found to make the platforms that would be the new one(s) to use.

There has been at least one attempt at a *FaceBook*

alternative—*Codias*. It has not taken hold. The interface is rather easy to use, certainly not a hindrance. No, it's failure to take hold has one obvious reason: it has billed itself as the conservative alternative. That is a killer. A look at the people on the platform shows that the vast majority of the users are over 50. Not the audience that is going to make a social media platform successful. A lesser concern is that it, like the one it hopes to displace, is secretive. There is no discernible way to contact anyone at *Codias*. Why the secrecy?

To make a successful run at the two big social media players, one would have to reach the millennials, and those under 50. Billing the platform as a conservative organization is a death knell, still, it would have to be, in order to get traction.

The platforms have to have a simple, but easy to

understand name. Deliver conservative ideas, as well as

factual news—and no one will notice that the stance is not

left. Deliver a well made, easy to use platform, one that

allows the free flow of ideas—all ideas--and it would be

successful.

To help that along the way, there must be legal

challenges and obstacles thrown in front of the big three of

social media.

Why you may rightly ask—has no one in the

government instructed the appropriate agencies to file anti-

trust lawsuits? Why has the government not rescinded the

special privileges and exemptions that these social media

platforms enjoy?

Call your GOP Congressman, party leader, and ask that

very question.

As a special note—there is now a twitter like service that

is gaining popularity—*Parler. Parler* (think "parlay") is

starting to find crossovers from twitter. Not many officials are on it, as of yet, but more are starting to use both Parler and Twitter. This should end any debate on whether or not a conservative platform can challenge the pre-existing and successful left leaning ones! Sign up for *Parler* now.

Take the initiative and start looking for a techie that can create a good, solid platform to challenge Facebook. *Parler* proves it can be done.

While *Google, FaceBook, and Twitter* are still the way most teens to young adults get their news, and hear "expert" opinions—some of that age group, and a lot of the 25 to 40 year olds, tune into a cable news outlet.

At the moment the cable universe is, like social media, the play ground of the socialist leftists. The news networks rail on about white racism, Republicans being racist. You have female *reporters* actually saying women have more rights under sharia, than they have in a Western Country. These same female reporters fawn over muslim leaders, and suggest that their listeners wear a hijab in solidarity of muslim women!

The only outlet, of a national level, that offered a conservative counterpoint was *Fox News*. A subtle change is beginning there, too. Over the last year, *Fox* has been adding leftist commentators. The last bastion of conservative opinion is going to the left.

While social media is of the utmost importance, we cannot ignore the cable news and opinions option. Conservatives have to make a presence here.

One approach would be to take over an existing cable TV station, convert it to a news channel. This channel could then be grown into a regional news outlet. Replicate this in keys areas, ex: one in the south, one in the northeast, and one in the west. These three stations, could combine resources, stories, to grow their individual footprints, and also put on a strong national front.

The pattern is rather the same that the old *Super Stations* used to come into prominence, decades ago. Will it cost money? Yes. Will it take time? Yes. Will it take dedication? Yes.

But, it is a necessity. The tide can be turned in a matter of months, to years, not decades—if we start now, and stick to the goal. Look at *aljazeera TV...* it started as, literally a mouthpiece for terrorist views, muslim apologist news. It still is that a decade later. But. It has been embraced by the mainstream media, other news channels, and often used as a source.

To get our message out there, we cannot rely on the

networks, social media, newspapers of today. We have to make sure outlets on all platforms are in place to get our message to the masses.

When there are outstanding voices in our community, ones that present conservative and moral views with clarity, and reason—we should make sure that those voices, opinions are heard. Some of the ones that come to mind, at present , include: Ben Shapiro, Candace Owens, Charlie Kirk, Dennis Prager, Micheal Knowles.

Ending the race baiting, rehabilitating a race

Since the election of 2008, and especially since the campaign for the 2016 presidency, race relations have taken a turn backwards.

Race baiters, some of whom were presidential advisers to the 2008/2012 president, are given free reign by the mainstream media to vilify one race—Caucasians. These same people, along with a willing media glorify racists of any other race – often calling on so called leaders of racist, violent groups to give their opinions on how to deal with the white race.

White kids in schools are being taught that the only way they, or any white person get ahead is due to the fallacy of *white privilege.*

In the 2020 race for President of the United States, all

of the Democrat candidates glorify *persons of color,* translation: any race that is not Caucasian. While the white candidates do a self-flagellation, and bemoan being white.

We have to end this cycle. Bring about balance again. Are there white racist? Most assuredly. Are there black racists? Most assuredly. Are there Hispanic racists? Most assuredly. Are there Asian racists? Most assuredly. To blame all racism on one race, is indeed, in of itself the very definition of racism.

To allow non-whites to use the term *persons of color* as a justification to be racist is asinine, and wrong. To allow anyone to be above suspicion, above reproach, because their skin tone is darker than another person's is not reverse racism—it is racism. Period.

We need to get back to the notion that you do not judge anyone based on the tone of their skin. We need to stop rewriting history. To teach, with pride the way our country was born, of the greatness of the founding fathers. To teach how the country went through the throws of dealing with racism, with slavery. *(It would be good to teach , on this subject that: there were white slaves—tens of thousands of them sold in the Middle-East; Irish that were brought to the United States as slaves; indentured servants, almost all were white, and due to debts, owned by the debt holders; that blacks were enslaved by other black nations, and muslim nations of northern Africa, and were then sold to Europeans... that Europeans did not go into Africa and randomly kidnap people)* How the civil rights movement was born, and of the great strides this country has made to become a nation of equal opportunity.

There is an urgent need to stop the segregation movements that our Universities and Colleges are pushing.

We must push back on the media/leftist notion that *"diversity"* is somehow more important than qualifications.

The then head of *Sam's Club*, was blatant about how she judged whether to do business with a company, based upon how many non-whites were on the board of directors. Not on the company's products, not on the qualifications of the board of directors—no, based solely on race. And that is the very definition of racism.

We have to blatantly point out, throw in anyone's face, that diversity is just a code for racism.

This goes for the constant use of a *person of color, by* non-whites, media, and politicians as a justification for hiring, electing, or believing someone. This is racism. Pure and simple.

The Political Arena

The socialist and communist left have seized control of the Democratic Party in the United States. To say otherwise is to bury one's head in the sand, so much as the old cartoon ostrich. They are consolidating that power, and using it to set the party's agenda.

We need to have a conservative party re-awakening. A third party option, while having merit, and being desired, is not a feasible option. With Ross Perot, it appeared that one might take flight, but it did not. Then came the *Tea Party*, but that too, turned out to be lip service only.

In the United States, at this moment in time, and in the foreseeable future, the only conservative player in the game is the Republican Party. Unfortunately, a Party that has proven to be ineffective, unmotivated, and unwilling to practice what it preaches. Examples? When the GOP controlled the White House and both houses of Congress, it failed to do simple things, such as defund Planned Parenthood, call for English as the United States official language, deal with the crisis of a porous Southern Border.

For years, weak willed, at best, Democratic Party members in disguise at worse, Republicans have failed the conservative movement. That has to change. It can.

In order to regain control of these United States, save the America that we now know, and love, we have to take control of political offices from the local offices to state offices to national offices.

Money, time, and attention has to be funneled into local Republican Party headquarters. Candidates have to be run in *all* local, and statewide races. A muslim won a state house race in Florida because not only did not another

Democrat run against him—but neither did one single

Republican! Such things cannot be allowed to happen.

The leadership of Florida's Republican Party should be

brought to task for this debacle.

To begin with, there has to be some vetting of

candidates: no, you cannot control who runs as Republican,

but you can choose which one(s) to back. In the 2020 race

for congress, many conservatives feel that they have to take

seats away from the leading socialists. Wise move—and

we'll get into that a little later—but, all ready the

Democrats are trying to water down the field of

challengers.

A woman entered the race against one of the leaders of

the socialism is the way movement, as a Republican. And

the media, as well as Republican leadership, went wild.

(the woman is a *person of color*) But just a quick look at her background and one finds: she is a follower of both Obama's. And, wrote a giddy congratulatory tweet to the very woman that she supposedly is running against.

Rejuvenation of the Party

The GOP needs a thorough cleansing from the local level through the state level, and especially the national level. Party members, leaders and candidates should be committed to conservative thoughts, and ready to work with and for the party's good.

How many Republican members of Congress have either left the party, or announced they will not run again, so far this year? Why? That is a question that needs to be asked, and answered.

At the local level there is a need to bring in new people,

younger members. We need to shake off a myth, quickly.

Namely that all young people are leftists, and have a

socialist bent. Says who? An effort has to be made to find

the next wave of conservatives, the next party leaders.

They are out there. We need to let them know we are here

for them, that they have a place. Putting a focused

mentoring program in place, one that reaches out to high

schoolers, Junior College and College/University students.

When it comes to local elections, emphasis should be

put on mayor and city council elections. After all, these

people not only set local agenda, they are where future

state and national leaders are plucked from.

Starting at the local level, and moving upwards,

conservatives need to steal a page from the Democrat's

playbook: running fake candidates, i.e..run at least one,

better--two or more Republicans as Democrats in the

Democratic Primaries! Why? This will dilute their primary, and, hopefully, draw votes away from their most popular candidates. On a best note—the fake Democrat will win the primary. On a cautionary note—you have to make sure the fake candidates are team players—that should they win, they will vote conservative.

This same sense of party has to permeate throughout the state leadership, as well. Candidates must be run in every state house race! In every state cabinet race! In every race for governor! Republican members must be run in all state wide races, as Republican, and as stealth Democrats.

What happened in Florida, where a Democrat won, unopposed cannot be allowed to happen.

So, how do you get one of your own to run as a member of the other party? You make sure he/she feels appreciated. That they are respected for taking on this task for the cause. One way to show that respect, and appreciation is to commit to running them in a future race, with the full backing of the party.

Now let's talk about a fallacy about *National* races. Other than President, no race is really national. Senate races are statewide, House of Representative races are local. You read that right.

Senate races are state wide, and each state has two senators. To win, keep control of the United States Senate, we need to stop relying on the *"we are strong here, there,"* which can work, with the right prioritizing and luck, and start running at least two strong candidates in each Senate race—our candidate as Republican, and at least one (two would be better) well known, articulate, likable candidate as a Democrat. Using our Democrat to attack the qualifications of the actual Democratic front runner.

To make this work, especially on the statewide platform, the stealth candidate has to be able to effectively come off as an actual member of that party. He or she cannot be seen coming to, leaving Republican Headquarters. If the stealth candidate has actually won a race as a Democrat, his or her credentials would appear beyond approach.

The races for House seats are done by local districts, often these districts have been drawn—by previous administrations to favor one party over the other. A district that has a Democrat in office, will generally go Democrat again, the same for the Republican side.

So, to win over a Democratic stronghold, and this is something we need to concentrate on, careful planning has to be used. In general, one would run the same type of program as you did in the races for US Senate and State House races, i.e..run at least one stealth candidate in the

Democratic Primary (again, two would be better).

However, there are some House races that would require

tweaking.

There are some Democrats in the House that the media

is fawning over, and telling the faithful that these are the

future leaders of that party. We need to take out as many of

these leftist darlings as possible.

But, you cannot go after them directly. No, if you

launch a full scale attack, the media will close ranks and

run hatchet pieces on the Republican challenger. He or

she will be branded a racist, a Nazi, a fascist—and those

will be the nicest thing said!

Here you need to run two challengers to the target in the

primary. One, that can pass the *progressive test*: free health

care for illegals; free college tuition for illegals. The other

should be on the extreme edge of leftism: not only free

health care for illegals, but also the most out there ideas feasible—open all borders; end the United States as a country; do away with all student loan debt. This candidate should be used to bring out negatives about the Democrat incumbent—should accuse the incumbent of being a socialist on paper only.

The idea is to appeal to the lunatic leftist fringe, show the incumbent's clay feet, and also to make those Democrats on the fence about socialist leanings, cringe and back away.

This way, all of the fighting, is amongst the Democrats. The press' s attention is focused on the warring Democrats, the negative stories are posted on that front. This leaves the field relatively clear for the Republican challenger.

The Sudden Success and Rise of Islam

In 2001 some three thousand citizens of the United States were obliterated. Another six thousand suffered injuries. Palestinians, upon hearing the news of thousands of Americans being killed, literally danced in the streets and threw block parties! (So why on earth do we send them hundreds of millions each year?) We vowed to never forget.

But we did forget. Not only did we forget, we allowed muslims to play the victim and race card! How? How did this happen? All it took was electing a muslim as President. And make no mistake about it, he is. Unless the videos have been pulled (and the may have, as YouTube, Twitter, and FaceBook are each pro islam), you can easily find him saying so.

In those eight years muslims were given key appointments in the president's cabinet, and used as advisers. Hillary Clinton's adviser, confidant, is a muslim with noted ties to the brotherhood.

Muslims were also given control of key parts of the Democratic National Party, and have effectively turned the Democratic Party into a de facto office of the muslim brother hood, or c.a.i.r—which is the North American brand of the brotherhood.

In the last Presidential race, astonishingly, the muslims were able to win over all of social media platforms and the national media by claiming victim hood—casting themselves as victims of hatred and of racism.

The leftists championed the muslims being victims—for they wanted their votes, but could only support them if they were somehow victims. So, anytime someone said muslims committed an act of terrorism—the Democrats immediately screamed, that muslims were being misjudged. And the press killed the story, and concentrated on some evil committed by a Christian, or Republican.

You had a female talking head on CNN telling her female audience members that they should all wear hijibs to show solidarity to muslim women. You had the press embracing muslims that openly called for the end of the Western World.

The Democrats, and the press went along with it, claimed that saying anything against islam was racist—even though islam is a religion—a set of rules, a thought process—most definitely not a race.

Hillary Clinton started using a word that the media ran with, and now all of the dictionaries, and social media platforms adhere to: i*slamaphobe*. Someone should remind these people, networks, platforms what exactly the word *phobia* means.

An irrational fear. There is nothing irrational about having apprehension, or even fear of a group that beheads people; says death is a justified punishment for leaving the faith; that says they are justified in killing anyone who draws a cartoon, disagrees with anything islamic.

C.A.I.R has stated that it is gearing up to run five thousand (you read that right, 5,000) muslims in political races throughout the United States. As previously noted one will soon be in the Florida State House, by virtue of not even being challenged!

The muslim brotherhood, having come to the conclusion that they were never again going to be able to take over Western Countries through force, changed tactics and came up with a plan to do so by destroying Western

Civilization from within. And, they are doing so.

An organization that helps veterans, through programs and placements, tried to run ads on Facebook. Being a Christian based group, one of the keywords they used was *"Christian."* Facebook rejected the ad. When questioned about it, Facebook replied that ads were not accepted that used any religious connotation. The veteran's help organization then tried an experiment—they placed the same ad, however they removed Christian from the keywords, but added *muslim*. The ad was accepted.

It is past time to fight back. By turning the other cheek, by ignoring what is happening, by being afraid of being called a racist—we, as a society, as a country have played right into the brotherhood's hands.

It is time for Christians to stop being naive about islam. It is time for Republicans , for conservatives to stop being naive about islam.

We have to take this threat seriously. We are letting hollywood, the media, and politicians who have money invested in the Middle-East, or are getting contributions from muslim countries, control the narrative.

When being interviewed by the media, and you are charged with being a racist and an islamaphobe—hit back. Call them out. "Well, you are the one who is racist—you are attacking me for my race—Christian (Jew, Wicca, etc). You are a Christianophobe! (it is a word) You Nazi, you are attacking me because of my race, my faith. How dare you..."

We must make sure atrocities that committed by muslims are covered, and looked at with horror. As you know the mainstream media covers these up now. This is why establishing our own platforms, and networks is imperative.

We must stop the wholesale entrance of muslim refugees... why are all of the people being brought over here as refugees muslim?.. there are Christians in the Middle-East, yet they never make it over here.

We must do away with welfare, benefits that are automatically given to refugees (and illegals, for that matter). U.S. Grant was noted as saying kill the enemy's food supply, and you will kill the enemy... This can, and should be applied with a twist. Stop the benefits, stop the free stuff, and they will stop coming.

We must flood the media, and platforms with pictures, stories of muslim extremism, of muslim clerics gloating that they will take over the United States. Of the muslim no go zones, of the third world looking areas of Paris, Berlin, Birmingham, London.

A Summary

The future of the United States, is in your hands. Sit on your behinds, keep turning the other cheek, keep saying it's up to someone else...

And, America will fall. Period. If not to the socialists, then to the ilsamists. As things are going now, I would say the country, unless we make a stand, will first go socialist, and in a decade or so, when it—like all socialist countries do—fails, the muslims will strike, and the world, for all intents and purposes will be a one religion shit show.

The Chinese Corona Virus and Shutdown

The Chinese unleashed a coronvirus on the world, got their lackeys at the WHO to cover for them for months.. Then when they saw it would be a grand way to take down the Western economy, they stalled more.

President Trump called them on this—the Chinese had the gall to say the virus was actually American made—and when he wouldn't back down, what happened? The Democratic Party started taking China's side! Of course the media joined in...China, the communist country that does not believe in human rights was now the victim of a racist President. Mind you, these democratic congressmen, and media geniuses couldn't figure out that Chinese is an ethnicity, not a race.

Democrats even introduced bills to make it illegal to refer to the Chinese coronavirus as, indeed, *Chinese*.

Then we had the Democrats and media insist that Trump use one Dr Fauci. This should have been a warning: a cursory check would have found his ties with Democrats, socialists. His mission seemed clear: doom and gloom. He pronounced that we should expect some two million deaths, that the *new normal* would be a US where everyone wore a mask, and obeyed government edicts.

Trump administration was all to eager to go along. The booming economy was shut down, people were wearing masks. Cheap masks that Fauci, and medical experts knew didn't work.

The economy in shambles, unemployment through the roof, the country is willing, at the moment to get back to work, to get back to normal.

But the democrats, globalists do not want this—they need to keep the economy on lockdown. To that end, Dr Fauci is once again screaming "doom & gloom," with predictions of 100,000 new cases per day! Oh, no! Now, you may remember that this is the guy who claimed there would be some one to two million Americans killed by the now called "covid-19" virus. Of course, that did not happen.

But the media is siding with the democrats and globalists again—railing on about the new cases, but failing to mention that hospitalizations have not gone up accordingly.

Their hypocrisy is unabashed: they say we must wear masks, and not be in any crowds—no church services, no family funerals, no concerts—yet, somehow the virus knew how to stay away from the funeral of George Floyd, stay away from all of the rioters...

We must break the cycle. Stand up to the wear a mask, keep away from each other, accept the new normal crowd. If a mask worked, then my not wearing one would not matter—because you are, and therefore you are protected!

We must be defiant. We must be bold. We must say

"Enough!"

President Trump has done a workman like response to

this "pandemic," but he has made enough missteps that the

media, in tandem with the DNC, will portray him as weak

and ineffective. He needs to make a bold stance. Push

back hard on the media.

Still, he need help from the rank and file, as well as the

conservatives who have been sitting this one out. We need

to start grass roots programs to show that his policies are

working. Hold classes, seminars for adults, teens and kids

(in disadvantaged areas, but more affluent ones as well) to

show them that this administration is neither weak, nor the

enemy.

Trump, and the GOP's biggest blunder, is the one that

just may cause his defeat in 2020, and end the United

States of America:

The Burning of America

The rise to power of the political party, Black Lives Matter is unparalleled. A remarkable achievement by the democrats, soros, and the media. And a disastrous blunder by President Trump, his advisers, and the Republican Party.

The declared "blm"--actually paid for thugs, bused in to destroy and terrorize—started to riot in burn down Minneapolis. The mayor, cheered it on. Two US members of congress from Minnesota cheered it on, and gloated at the carnage and lack of response from the President.

The democrat strategists saw no response from the President, or there republican counter parts—noted the glee of the college/university students and faculty; the rush to make the rioters heroes by the media, and major corporations—and put this into overdrive.

Emboldened, the rioters/looters were organized and sent to cities across the nation: Seattle, Portland, Tampa, new york, Atlanta... Democratic mayors, governors turned a blind eye.

The democrat/soro's creation was organized and injected into England, Europe, Australia. BLM in little more than a month had become the most powerful political party on earth.

Yet the President, either on his own, or listening to clueless advisers—did nothing. He let cities burn. He let the house of representative members laugh at him, dare him to challenge them. The media portrayed the rioters as heroes fighting an evil USA for "racial" justice.

The GOP, conservatives, churches did nothing to fight this narrative. By cowering, we now find ourselves having our lives, our livelihood dictated, decided by a racist, violent 5% of a 15% minority.

Trump should not just have spoken out about this rioting, looting, burning of cities when it happened. At the very first instance, in Minneapolis, he should have responded—by executive decision sent in the military to restore peace, and to take into custody of the criminals.

But he did not. Whether through indifference, or listening to advisers. He let the blm grow from a local blip to a national movement, and finally into a worldwide power.

BLM is now so powerful that if you speak out against hem they will tell your employer to fire you—and the cowardly, all too eager to be "non-racist" will do so!

Corporate america is in full swing behind this movement. Disney has just given colin kapernick millions to produce show for them. Any guess on what the show will be "teaching9' your children and grandchildren? Netflix dropped millions to obama to make shows—once again on the evil whites, and, of course pro muslim.

What was, is the response form President Trump, GOP, "religious leaders?" Silence. But then, what has been the response, the push back from the majority of US citizens? The same. Nothing.   Silence.

Now the governors, mayors are demanding that Trump rebuild what the democrat/soros created blm party destroyed. He should not. He should call it a local and state affair. Tell them to bill BLM.

You should get off of your keyster, call your congressman, and tell them that you are not going to pay, through taxes, to rebuild what racist, terrorists destroyed.

If you sit this out. Kiss your freedom good-bye. Kiss the United States of America, good-bye.

I am always open to queries, and questions. Feel free to

contact me: chchra@outlook.com   wstaggs@live.com

God Bless America

Best wishes to you, and yours!